My Short E Words

Consultants

Ashley Bishop, Ed.D.
Sue Bishop, M.E.D.

Publishing Credits

Dona Herweck Rice, *Editor-in-Chief*
Robin Erickson, *Production Director*
Lee Aucoin, *Creative Director*
Sharon Coan, *Project Manager*
Jamey Acosta, *Editor*
Rachelle Cracchiolo, M.A.Ed., *Publisher*

Image Credits

cover Rey Kamensky/Shutterstock; p.2 Rey Kamensky/Shutterstock; p.3 CLM/Shutterstock; p.4 Ruslan Kudrin/Shutterstock; p.5 Boleslaw Kubica/Shutterstock; p.6 Phant/Shutterstock; p.7 Christophe Testi/Shutterstock; p.8 kali9/istockphoto.com; p.9 karam Miri/Shutterstock; p.10 Lasse Kristensen/Shutterstock; back cover CLM/Shutterstock

Teacher Created Materials

5301 Oceanus Drive
Huntington Beach, CA 92649-1030
http://www.tcmpub.com

ISBN 978-1-4333-2563-2

© 2012 Teacher Created Materials, Inc.

I like the elephant

I like the bell.

I like the dress.

I like the desk.

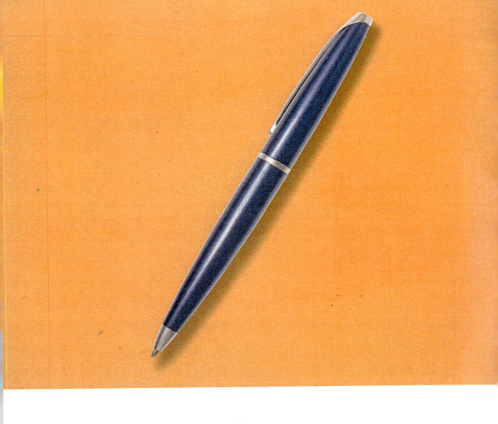

I like the pen.

I like the pencil.

I like the vet.

I like the tent.

I like the lettuce.

Glossary

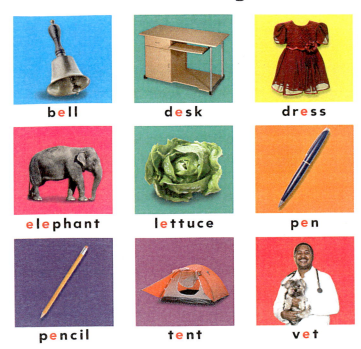

bell	desk	dress
elephant	lettuce	pen
pencil	tent	vet

Sight Words

I   like   the

Activities

- Read the book aloud to your child, pointing to the short *e* words as you say them. After reading each page, ask, "What do you like?"

- Have your child help you organize a desk at your home. Remind him or her that the word *desk* has the short *e* sound. Discuss the importance of staying organized with your child and how a desk can help you do that.

- Make a colorful salad with your child using lettuce and different types of vegetables and then share it for lunch.

- Challenge your child to say the word *veterinarian* five times as fast as possible.

- Help your child think of a personally valuable word to represent the short *e* sound, such as *leg*.